A Country Journal

Illustrated With the
Writings of
David Grayson

Being a Collection of the Thoughts,
Observations and Engagements of:

541 Oak St. ~ P.O. Box 177
Frederick, CO 80530

ISBN: 1-55838-113-9

Copyright ©1989 by Renaissance House Publishers. Printed in the United States of America. All rights reserved. This book or any parts thereof, may not be reproduced in any manner whatsoever without the written permission of the publisher:

RENAISSANCE HOUSE PUBLISHERS
A Division of Jende-Hagan, Inc.
541 Oak Street ~ P.O. Box 177
Frederick, CO 80530

A COUNTRY JOURNAL
is a compilation of quotations from
eight major books by David Grayson:

Adventures in Contentment   **The Countryman's Year**
Adventures in Friendship   **Under My Elm**
Adventures in Understanding   **Great Possessions**
Adventures in Solitude   **The Friendly Road**

All books are now or will soon be available from
Renaissance House Publishers
For information Call Toll Free 1-800-521-9221

Publisher's Foreword

"I have always liked best," said David Grayson, "books that have been lived before being written. It is not experience alone that makes a man interesting to himself or to his neighbors, but the afterthoughts and transmutations." With that in mind, Grayson recorded in small notebooks "comments upon books I read, people I met and, above all, the things I meditated upon as I went about doing the quiet work of my land, my orchard and my bees."

This Journal is your chance to do the same. We offer it as a diary, an engagement calendar, a log book, a guest register, or what have you. Use it to record special thoughts or events in your life: baby's first word or big brother's first day at school, jottings about your garden, birds you have spotted, wines you have enjoyed, meaningful quotations, synopses of good books, plays, films, recordings.

You will find your Journal loosely structured around a calendar year, but without notation of specific days and months. This design is an attempt to accommodate each of us: those whose daily observations overfill a 2x4-inch slot, as well as those of us who write in Journals on a sporadic basis.

The "Commonplace Book" of days-gone-by was a book in which the author recorded noteworthy poems, quotations, comments and the like. This is your commonplace book, illustrated by David Grayson. Enjoy and treasure it.

David Grayson has been my faithful companion for over twenty years. I discovered him, much as Renaissance House "rediscovered" him, on a dusty bookshelf in New England. Subsequently I searched for copies of all his books. I have read and re-read, ear-marked, highlighted and taken notes -- even classified the lyrical quotations so I could make them my own, to be called upon at appropriate times to satisfy a moment or describe my feelings.

David himself asserts that "every great book either makes us want to do things -- or it takes us out of ourselves and beguiles us for a time with the friendship of completer lives than our own."[1]

He believed that "all great writing of whatsoever kind, somehow releases the soul of man, the poor caged spirit seeking some balm for the brevity of life, some friend for the loneliness of it, some strength for the weakness of it."[2]

Like David, I am a "besotted reader," a book collector, given to "making anthologies of ourselves."[3] "Whenever words fly up to me, I intercept them instantly, knowing they are for me. I turn them over carefully in my mind and cling to them hard. Sometimes I commit them to memory or copy them down as a permanent possession, often to be taken out for my pleasure, thought about, gloated over."[3]

"I do not want long books, but scraps and extracts and condensations from which thoughts can be plucked like flowers and carried for awhile in the buttonhole." [4] For (Grayson continues) "if men are made up largely of what they select as they go through life, these passages I have so gladly intercepted not only represent what I admire or what I like, they are in reality a part of Me, myself."[3]

Although I have not weighed whether David Grayson's life was "completer" than mine (and he'd be the first to dispute it himself), I find in his writings "expressions of a life much occupied in other employment."[1]

All of these selected quotations are offered, as Grayson offered his writing, to "somehow help people to go on living, or enduring, or enjoying; they all, somehow, express ideas or emotions which are dimly their own, for which they have no adequate words."[3]

David's observations on happiness, contentment, country living, nature, the seasons, friends, neighbors and mankind, as well as his wisdom, abound in every chapter of his books. He reminds us that "in the long run, no writing survives that is not useful or helpful to some human being."[3] Which is why I affirm: David Grayson is timeless!

Joan F. Pegram
Jupiter, Florida

(1) Adventures in Contentment
(2) The Countryman's Year
(3) Under My Elm
(4) Great Possessions

Renaissance House is grateful to Joan Pegram
for her sensitive and thoughtful selection
of the quotes which grace the pages of
A Country Journal

Contents

DESCRIPTION	PAGES

DESCRIPTION	PAGES

Winter

Winter is the true time for indoor enjoyment! Days like these! A cold night after a cold day! Well wrapped, you have made arctic explorations to the stable, the chicken-yard and the pig-pen, stopping every few minutes to beat your arms around your shoulders and watch the white plume of your breath in the still air -- and you have rushed in gladly to the warmth of the dining-room and the lamp-lit supper. After such a day how sharp your appetite, how good the taste of food!

A lamp with a green shade stands invitingly on the table shedding a circle of light on the books and papers underneath, but leaving all the remainder of the room in dim pleasantness... Let the wind blow outside and the snow drift in piles around the doorway and the blinds rattle -- I have before me a whole long pleasant evening.
Adventures in Contentment

"Git up there!" he called to his horses, and in a moment we were whirling up the road -- the sun glinting on the shining brasses of the harness and the red pompons dancing on the horses' heads. Occasionally a ball of snow cast by the horses' hoofs would come whirling back into the sled, and the sunny air was full of fine, sharp ice crystals that stung our faces or felt like pepper in our nostrils. And all about, sunshine and wide snowy fields, and a sky above as blue and clear as a man

ever saw. Who can describe such a winter day! How it makes the blood race in one's veins and all the earth appear inexpressibly beautiful.
Adventures in Understanding

*I*t was a perfect sugar day. Last night it froze hard, and today the sun shines warm: and every one of the hundreds of trees that have been tapped are dripping sap into shining pails that hang from the spiles.

The sap is boiled in long shallow pans heated by a roaring fire of four-foot wood, there being a gradual flow from the pan where the sap comes in from the vat to the deeper pans where the syrup begins to grow thick and is of a deep golden color.
The Countryman's Year

It is idle to consider whether what you have to give, whether you yourself, are of any use or importance to the world. Be it, give it; it is all you have. No one was ever yet able to fix his own price: this is determined, like that of any other commodity, by the demand. Some people will want what you have or what you are, and some will not. It is a market that can sometimes be rigged temporarily: never for long.

The Countryman's Year

Is it not a fine Providence that gives us different things to love? In the purchase of my farm both Horace and I got the better of the bargain -- and yet neither was cheated. In reality a fairly strong lantern light will shine through Horace, and I could see that he was hugging himself with the joy of his bargain; but I was content. I had some money left -- what more does anyone want after a bargain? -- and I had come into possession of the thing I desired most of all.   **Adventures in Contentment**

*T*he joy of winter: the downright joy of winter! ...I tramped today through miles of it: and whether in broken roads or spotless fields, had great joy of it... The spring is beautiful indeed, and one is happy at autumn, but of all the year no other mornings set the blood to racing like these; none gives a greater sense of youth, strength or the general goodness of the earth. Give me the winter: give me the winter! Not all winter, but just winter enough, just what nature sends. **Great Possessions**

I could sit here this wintry morning and write a poem -- or an essay -- or possibly a book! -- on the joy of an open fire, such as I have burning here upon my hearth. It is the soul of the house: the center of its joy, the inspiration of its labor. Said Aretino, that scandalous old blackguard of the Italian renaissance:

"Four dry logs have in them all the circumstance necessary to a conversation of four to five hours... Yes, let us love winter, for it is the spring of genius."

The Countryman's Year

My years fall away on a day like this. On a day like this I take part of my immortality... This morning I was out at sunrise. A few fleecy pink clouds floated high in the heavens, and every tree cast a rich blue shadow. The air was sharp and frosty -- infinitely exhilarating... If one could imagine himself living <u>inside</u> of a diamond and that diamond full of sunlight -- radiated and reflected from every facet, sparkling upon every point until the glory was bewildering -- it would give a poor idea of what this morning has been like. **The Countryman's Year**

One who comes thus to love a bit of countryside may enjoy it all the year round. When he wakens in the middle of a long winter night, he may send his mind out to the snowy fields -- I've done it a thousand times! -- and visit each part in turn, stroll through the orchard and pay his respects to each tree... stop at the strawberry bed, feel himself opening the door of the warm, dark stable and listening to the warming whicker of his horses, or visiting his cows, his pigs, his sheep, his hens... **Great Possessions**

This winter an extraordinary number of crows have wintered near us in the marshes... I have enjoyed watching them. Today I examined their tracks in the snow: not clean-cut, but dabbled with the marks of wing and tail feathers. One old crow -- there seems to be but one that does it -- sets the four front toes of each foot down like a mitten, three together and one separate: I suppose that crows are as different as human beings, if one could come to know them.

The Countryman's Year

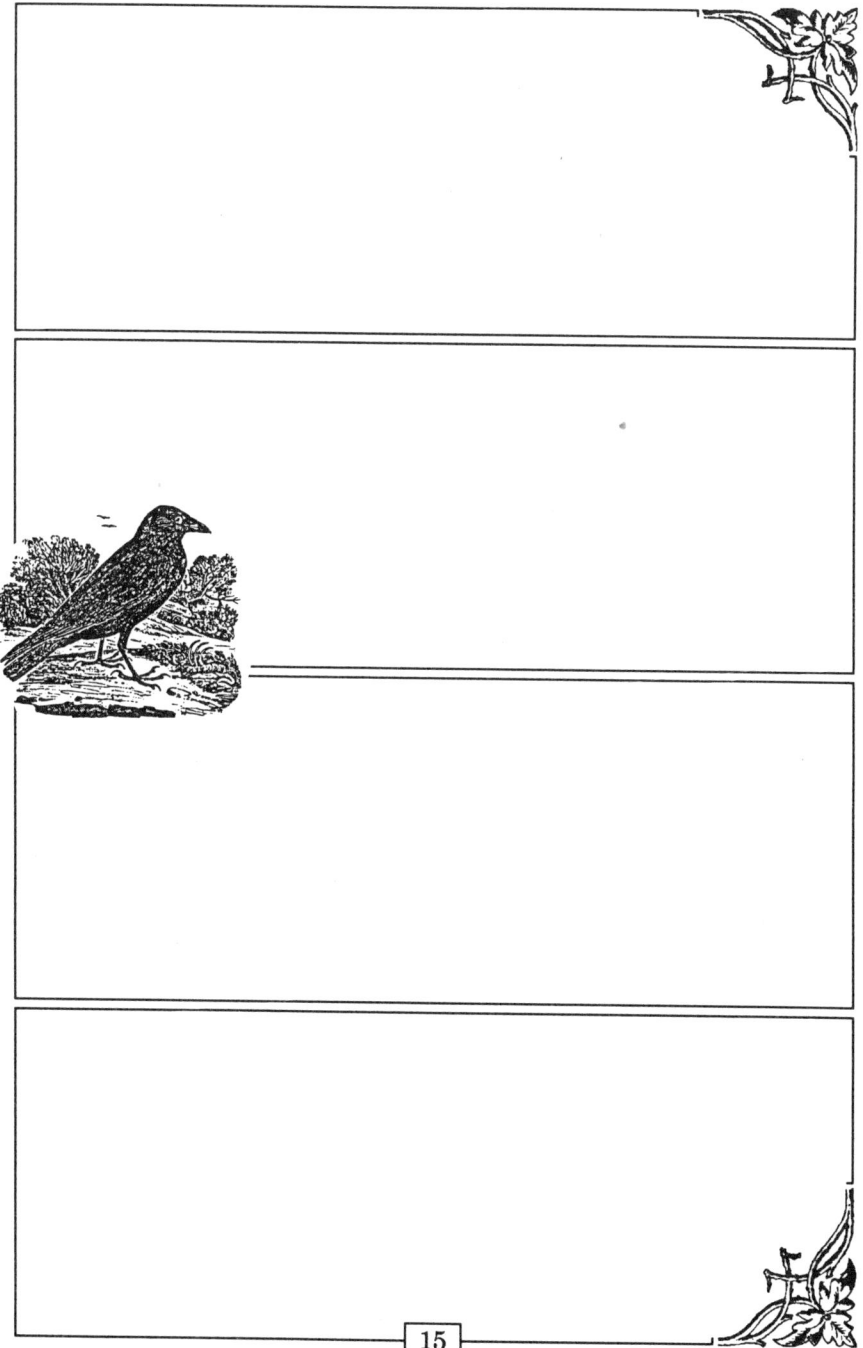

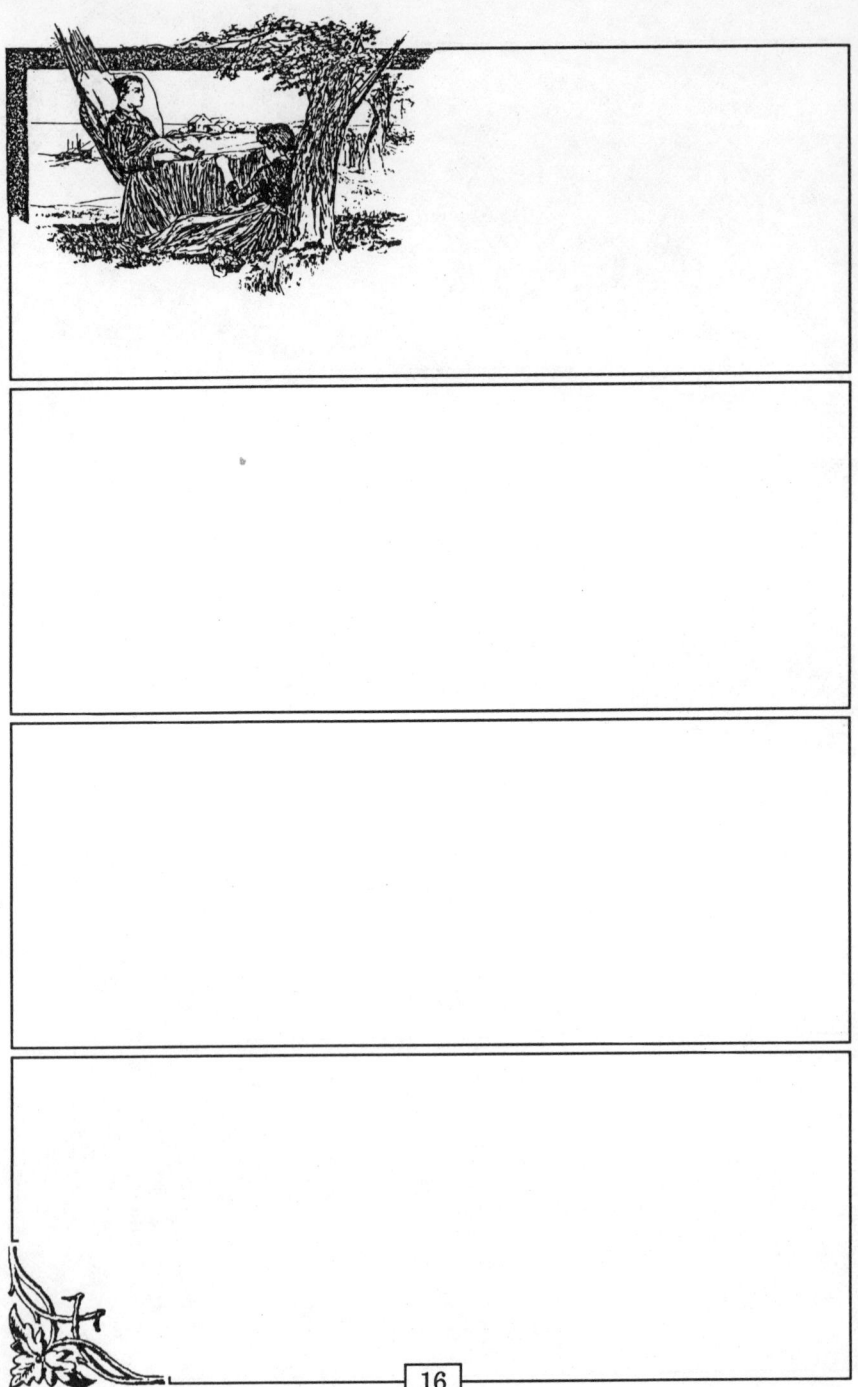

It so often happens that when a man has reached the point where he feels he is beginning to know how to command his life and the tools of his employment, to reap the harvest of his labour, tragedy of one sort or another touches him on the shoulder... While it was true that everything that had constituted a pleasant and satisfying life for me...had been stripped away, I was still possessed of my mind and my own thoughts. I had, after all, my own inner life. I had my life!

Adventures in Solitude

> *For years I had been secretly longing for quiet, for retirement, for a chance to think... Well, I now had my desires involuntarily fulfilled... and I was not content. It was not an easy matter, even after I had discovered the true secret and place of my possessions, that they were inward, to enter upon their enjoyment or use them as a sure way to tranquillity... I and none other was the architect of my felicity.*
>
> **Adventures in Solitude**

There is loneliness on a long voyage, even to one who has learned in some measure to live in the house of his own spirit -- and one turns with eagerness to his fellow passengers. Strange men and women whom he has never seen before, nor heard of, and yet they are somehow bound to him and he to them by the common experiences and dangers of the voyage... It is like that greater and sometimes painful voyage on the good ship Earth...

Adventures in Solitude

A remarkable springlike day, full of sunshine and running water -- and a hungry unrest of the spirit. I could not think of work, but of...the young things of the woods peeping out to see if winter is over and gone. I think I never saw the sky so high and clear, or ever knew the winds so sweet... It seems to me I have had much joy of this day, and many pleasant thoughts. And I have not worked at all, and am not sorry, either; for there are days when it is well that a man should let the quiet of nature completely fill his soul. **The Countryman's Year**

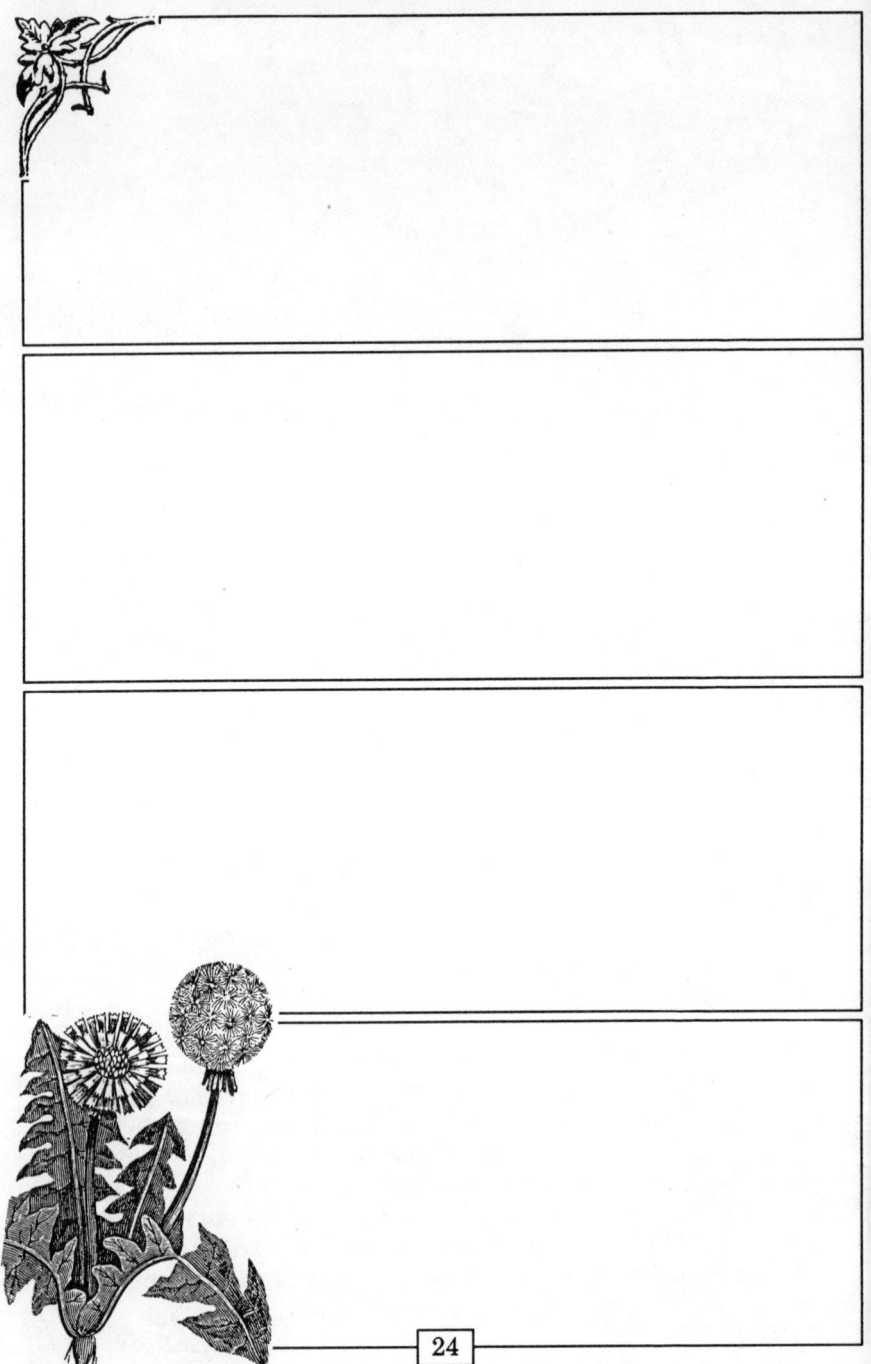

*T*oday, in the marshes, I saw the first of the skunk cabbages thrusting their way upward from the sedgy brookside... There was nothing strange or newly beautiful about them...yet those cowled heads rising from the slime of the marsh, seeking the sunshine of spring, gave me such a thrill as I cannot describe. It seemed suddenly and greatly beautiful to me, the patience of nature... Whatever happens, it endures: year after year for inconceivable millions of years: and never discouraged!

The Countryman's Year

Surely the chief delight of going away from home is the joy of getting back again. I shall never forget that spring morning when I walked from the city of Kilburn into the open country... I remember how eagerly I looked out across the fields and meadows and rested my eyes upon the distant hills. How roomy it all was! ...There was space to breathe, and distances in which the spirit might spread its wings.

The Friendly Road

Spring

*O*ne day -- it was in April, I remember, and the soft maples in the city park were just beginning to blossom -- I stopped suddenly. I did not intend to stop. I confess in humiliation that it was no courage, no will of my own. I intended to go on toward Success: but Fate stopped me. It was as if I had been thrown violently from a moving planet: all the universe streamed around me and past me. It seemed to me that of all animate creation, I was the only thing that was still or silent. Until I stopped I had not known the pace I ran.

Adventures in Contentment

*T*he perfections of a New England trout brook! Hills above clad with birches and great old hemlocks, ferns crowding so near the water that their fronds dipped in, the stream itself full of old round boulders, and pools, and eddies, and delightful little gravel bars where one could stand to cast into the stream below. And the music of it all, and the sunshine of a morning in May... No, there is no excuse for fishing except joy.

Under My Elm

*I*t was June. I had come out after supper to sit on my porch and look out upon the quiet fields. I remember the grateful cool of the evening air, and the scents rising all about me from garden and roadway and orchard. I was tired after the work of the day and sat with a sort of complete comfort and contentment which comes only to those who work long in the quiet of outdoor places. I remember the thought came to me, as it has come in various forms so many times, that in such a big and beautiful world there should be no room for the fever of unhappiness or discontent.

Adventures in Friendship

I am firmly convinced that the happiest men I know have their feet -- or at least one foot -- in the soil... Country life is not to be taken by storm: nor happiness acquired by moving into a farmhouse. And yet I know many instances in which the world has been changed for human beings by going to live in a garden, or by cultivating a few rods or acres of land as part of a life occupied with other things.
The Countryman's Year

I have worked hard all the week: and have now a blessed moment of rest... I came here to a little valley I know among the trees... I can hear the wind, like distant surf, rolling in the forest tops, but where I sit, it is still and warm: and all the air pungent with the smell of pine needles. The crows are nesting in their rookery. I can hear their intimate conversation... How still it all is. Spring seems truly here at last.

The Countryman's Year

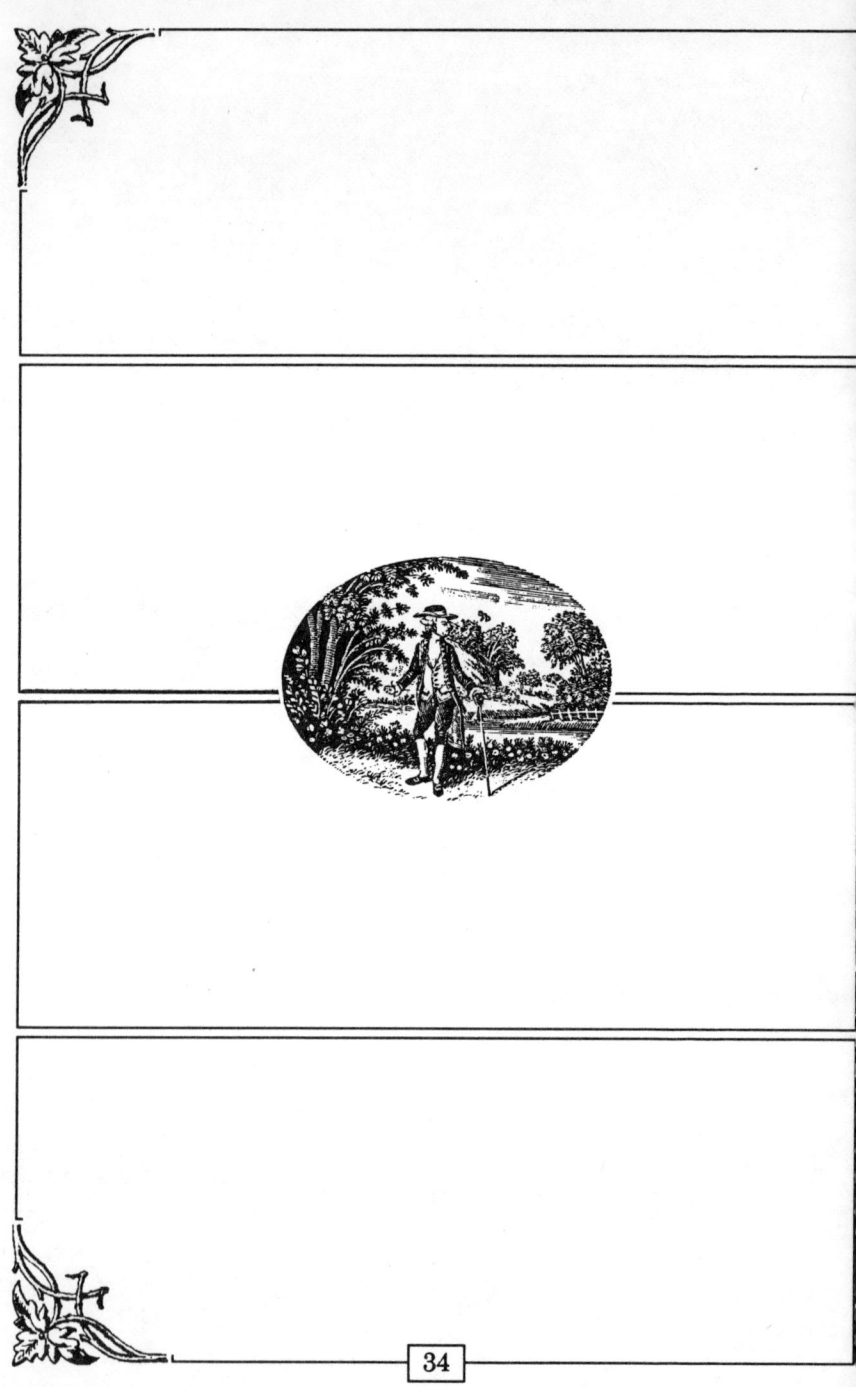

*O*n a spring morning one has only to step out into the open country, lift his head to the sky -- and follow his nose... It was a big golden morning...and I walked down the lane to the lower edge of the field, where the wood and the marsh begin. The sun was just coming up over the hills and all the air was fresh and cool.... It seemed to me that morning that the world was...filled to the brim with the essence of sunshine and spring morning -- so that one's spirit dissolved in it, became a part of it. Such a morning!

Great Possessions

I was reminded today, as so often before, of the continuity and permanence of nature. All the sights I saw, the sounds I heard, came in upon me as in every spring I ever knew before. And in every spring of future years, whether I am here or not, there will be the same glow of red maples in the marsh...the same blooming daffodils, the same robins in wide, green meadows, and flashing bluebirds in old fence corners. All the sweet repetition of the symphony of spring.

The Countryman's Year

I know I use too many exclamation points, but the fact is, I am so astonished by some of the things I see and hear of a spring morning that it is only an exclamation point that will relieve my feelings... Lifting off thought after thought I know well where my joy is: in things still and scenes quiet, in days like these in May in our own valley, in my bees, in my orchard, in the thrushes and catbirds I hear singing, in the flash of a bluebird's wing. These I love: these quiet my soul.

Under My Elm and The Countryman's Year

It was May in the City, and where is May not beautiful? The vines were coming freshly green on old walls, the elms were showing their new soft verdure...and in many a friendly window I could see the beckoning welcome of potted daffodils or narcissus... I looked in at curious alleys and openings as I passed, and old area-ways and strange nooks and corners. I love such irregularities, unexpected passageways; the odd shifts of human beings to meet the small difficulties of life.
Adventures in Understanding

I liked, at once, the old street and the old house with the lichens of human living upon it... I like such places: old quiet places, places to look out of; old, still, sunny places and beautiful people going by...windows that have been much looked through; rooms full of thoughts left over out of life... Here men have dreamed and women loved... Something, I scarcely know what, but it is real, seems to remain of all human contact. Nothing human is ever wholly lost. **Adventures in Understanding**

I spent a considerable part of this sunny afternoon trying to get a good look at a pair of Maryland yellow-throats which have recently arrived in our neighborhood. They are easy to hear, often hard to see. ...So I sat there on the hillside and waited. So many times in my life I have had things I desired not by seeking but by waiting. Presently I heard the shy singer again: "Witchery, witchery, witchery." Witchery it is, I said aloud, and turned homeward.

The Countryman's Year

I was up at sunrise and went out into the dewy world -- long shadows on the grass, the sun just touching the treetops, as fine a June morning as ever I saw in my life... There was a faint scent from somewhere up the hill -- the mock oranges, I think -- and I could see, not far away, the heavy pink peonies of the flower garden in heavy bloom. It was still, still, scarcely a bird note -- for the early morning concert was past -- but far off across the valley I could hear the rumble of a farm wagon.

The Countryman's Year

Of all the trees that ever I knew, I have loved none better than my elm... The meadow on which the elm stood did not belong to us, but we had our harvests of beauty from it year after year as though it were our own... I was finally able to purchase outright the meadow where the tree stands. It is now, of course, no more my elm than it was before -- but I now hold the silly bit of paper which makes me at once the arbiter and the sharer of the noblest tree in the countryside.

Under My Elm

> *One who takes part in the whole process of the year comes soon to have an indescribable affection for his land, his garden, his animals. There are thoughts of his in every tree: memories in every fence corner. Just now, the fourth of June, I walked down past my blackberry patch... I set out these plants with my own hands, I have fed them, cultivated them, mulched them, pruned them, trellised them, and helped every year to pick the berries. How could they be otherwise than full of associations!*
> **Great Possessions**

*J*oy of life seems to me to arise from a sense of being where one belongs... of being foursquare with the life we have chosen. All the discontented people I know are trying sedulously to be something they are not, to do something they cannot do... It is curious, is it not... with how little wisdom we farm the soils of our own natures. We try to grow poetry where plumbing would thrive grandly! -- not knowing that plumbing is as important and honourable and necessary to this earth as poetry.

Adventures in Friendship

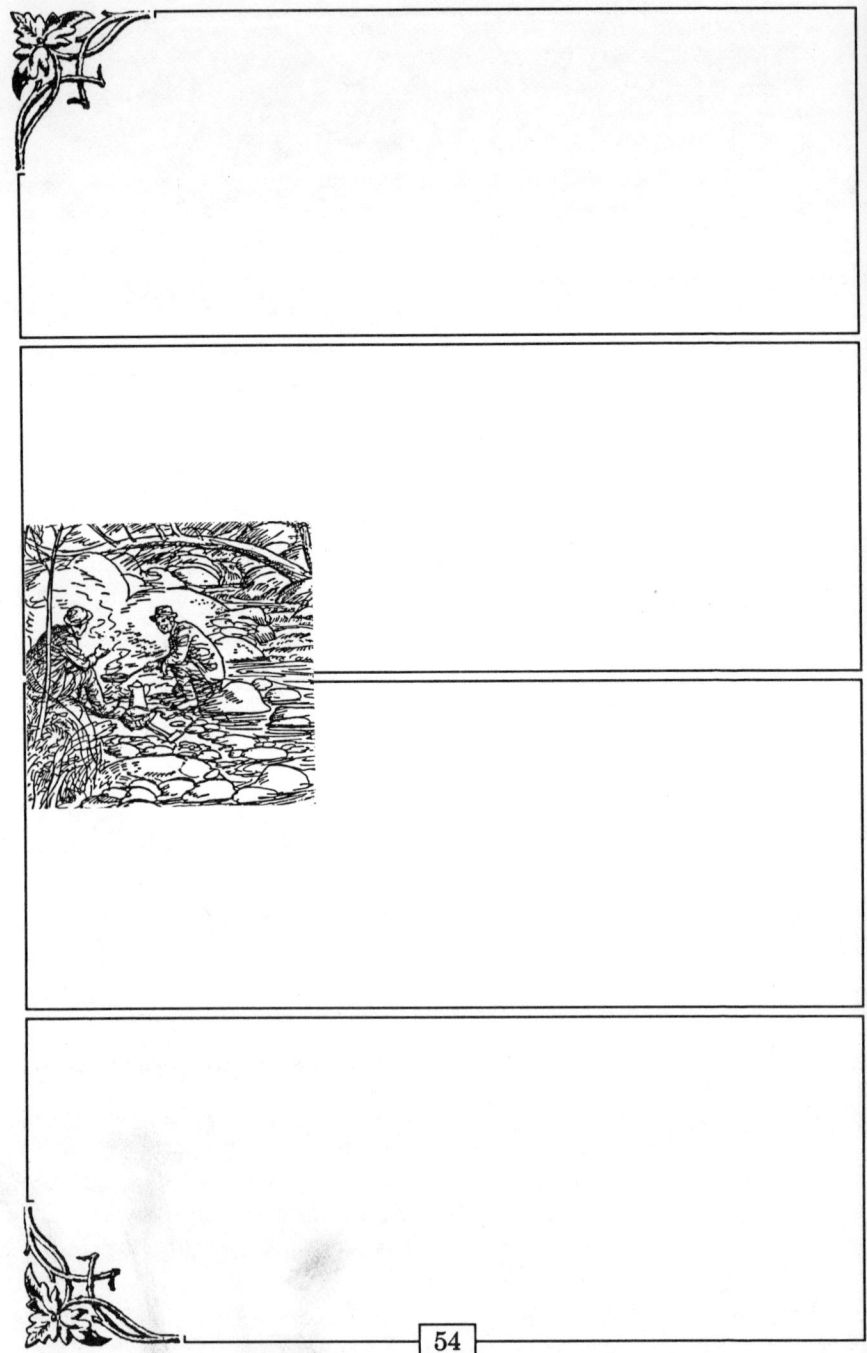

When I left home on Friday morning I had put aside several knotty problems. I had put them away in the warm deep places of the mind. While I was not looking, that day on Barrus Brook, the sunshine somehow got into them, and the clear air, and the music of the water among the stones and the blossoming shadbushes, and the birds -- and when the next morning I had my problems out again, there they were, quite clear and simple, no more perplexities.

Under My Elm

Summer

*M*ornings *like this, it seems, there is nothing that is not possible: nothing I do not believe. I look about the earth and the heavens: there is not <u>enough</u> to believe -- mornings like this. ...You will go by, in coming years, you will go by and never know that I was here: that here in this sunny field upon this hillside I was hot and hard and evil, I was possessive and passionate here; I saw beauty here, and loved... You will go by and I shall not be here.*

The Countryman's Year

I thought much in the long days of my illness how impossible it was for any human being to live without faith -- faith somewhere, in something, in somebody. All that makes a man a man and not an animal is suffused with faith. Without it the individual is insane and society a chaos. With it, and in proportion to the vitality of it, there can be nobility, and peace, and serenity

Adventures in Solitude

*T*here is a kind of sturdy humour in the country that the city does not know. A humour that grows straight out of the soil. There may be wit in the city, but wit deals with words: humour with life. I was amused at Horace's observation regarding his visit to the City, when he spent a holiday with us. He had enjoyed every minute of it, said he; but, "I was glad to git home again where people understand my jokes." (Humour, when you come to think of it, is the very last thing we come to understand in a foreign place or a foreign language.)

Adventures in Understanding

It has been hot and dry... But last night came the rain... There was not a breath of wind... It was as though nature had drawn a long sigh...and had begun to weep softly, copiously... It came straight down and filled all the night with comfort and release... From time to time the downpour slackened, and then I heard the dripping among the trees and from the eaves of the house, like hushed voices telling one another sleepily of their joy... but never a word could I make out, but knew it was all in verse: the poetry of the rain. **The Countryman's Year**

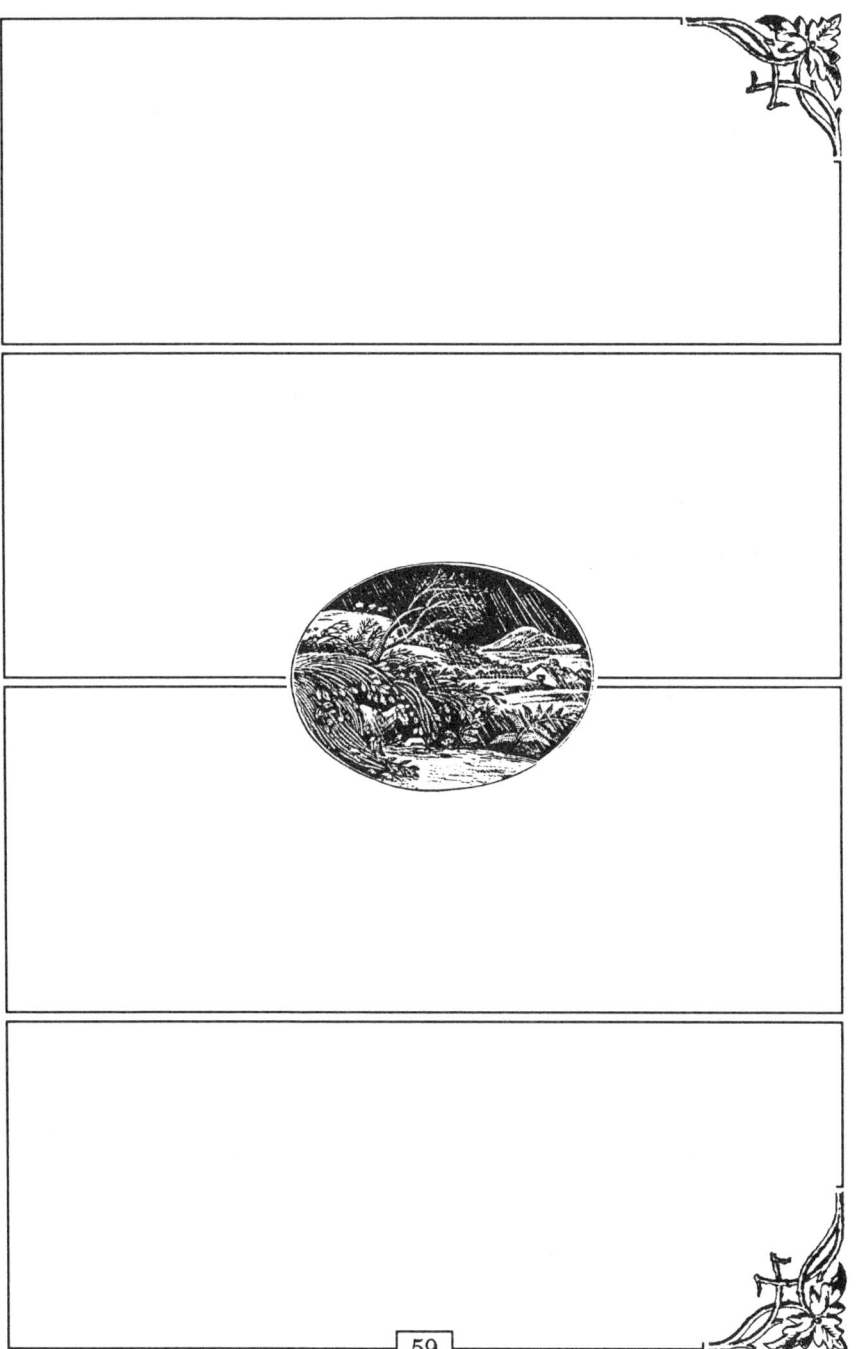

I have always believed that men in their innermost souls desire the highest, bravest, finest things they can hear, or see, or feel in all the world. Tell a man how he can increase his income and he will be grateful to you and soon forget you; but show him the highest, most mysterious things in his own soul and give him the word which will convince him that the finest things are really attainable, and he will love and follow you always.

The Friendly Road

You may know the true gardener by his willingness to kneel in the earth -- He loves the feel of the soil: he loves to step around in his garden paths in such warm moist mornings of July as this, when vegetation can almost be seen to grow. He loves every row of corn, every hill of melons, every clump of tall hollyhocks: and because he loves, he disciplines, prunes, thins.

The Countryman's Year

As I grow older I remain here on my farm, and wait quietly for the world to pass this way. My oak and I, we wait, and we are satisfied. Here we stand among our clods; our feet are rooted deep within the soil. The wind blows upon us and delights us, the rain falls and refreshes us, the sun dries and sweetens us. We are become calm, slow, strong; so we measure rectitudes and regard essentials, my oak and I.

Adventures in Friendship

It is the still middle age of the year: the time of sunny fullness, of harvest, of fulfillment. I have been working, writing, thinking. I let the world go by... I walk alone across the fields...and sit in the still woods. I tramp onward to the wide meadow...looking out upon the hazy beauty of that summer scene -- the glint of river, blue hills beyond, and the roofs of the little town among the foliage... It seems to me I want now to be quiet for a century or so to consider all the things I have ever seen or heard or felt or thought.

The Countryman's Year

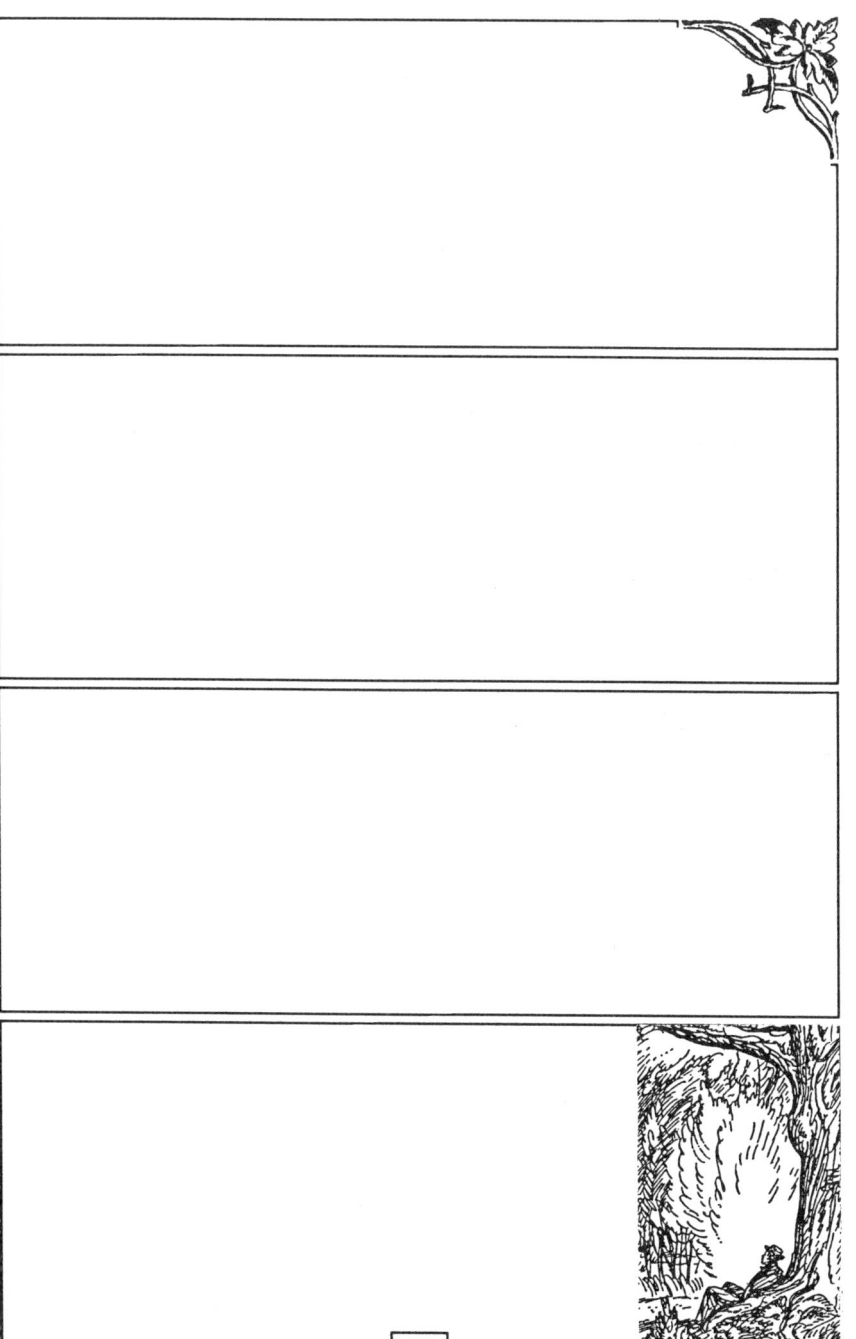

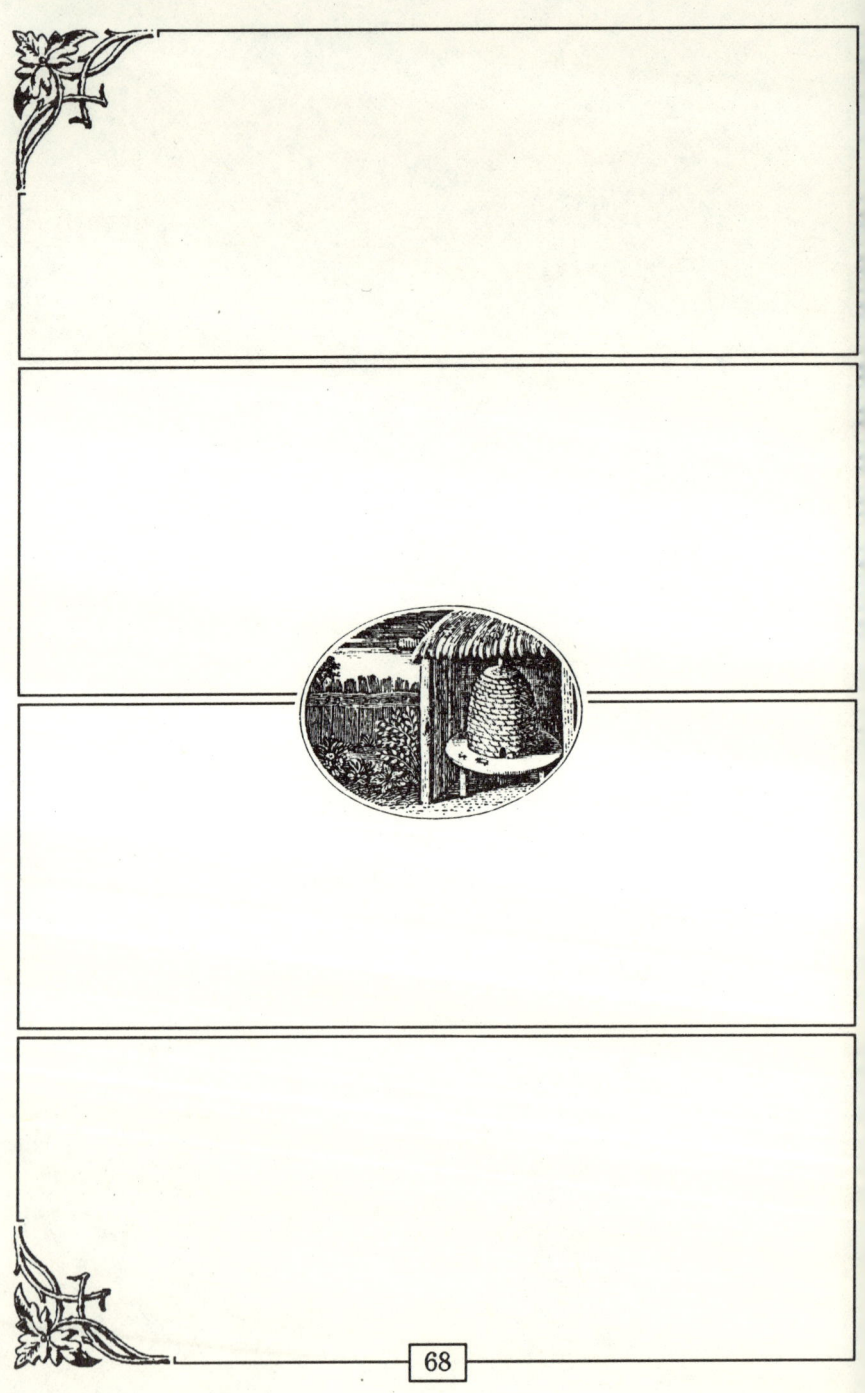

If only everyone could get his feet somewhere, somehow, down into the soil... It may not be your only work; you may wish to teach Greek or write novels or make butter bowls or work in a garage, but somewhere, somehow, each day get back to your own garden or trees or bees or grass plot -- even a pot of tulips in the window! ...It will not of itself make men happy or peaceful, but it will help... It is a way toward reality: it links the soul of man with the creative spirit.

The Countryman's Year

A certain old barn I love well. A great, gray old barn, reaching out its sheds like wings on either side to hover the cattle when they come in at evening... I love the cavernous open doorway where the barn swallows fly chittering in and out. I love the dusty smell of hay as I step inside... From within, looking out, I can see the pleasant rolling country, fine fields and verdure-clad hills, with the sun upon them. There is no frame made by man that can equal the doorway of this barn, and no picture anywhere so well worth the framing.

Adventures in Solitude

How surely, soundly, deeply, the physical underlies the spiritual. This morning I was up and out at half-past four, as perfect a morning as I ever saw: mists yet huddled in the low spots, the sun coming up over the hill, and all the earth fresh with moisture, sweet with good odours, and musical with early bird-notes... After hastening with the chores...I walked in the cool broad shadows. On my left stretched the cornfield of my planting... I looked up and about me -- not to miss anything of the morning -- and thought the world had never been so open to my senses.   **Adventures in Contentment**

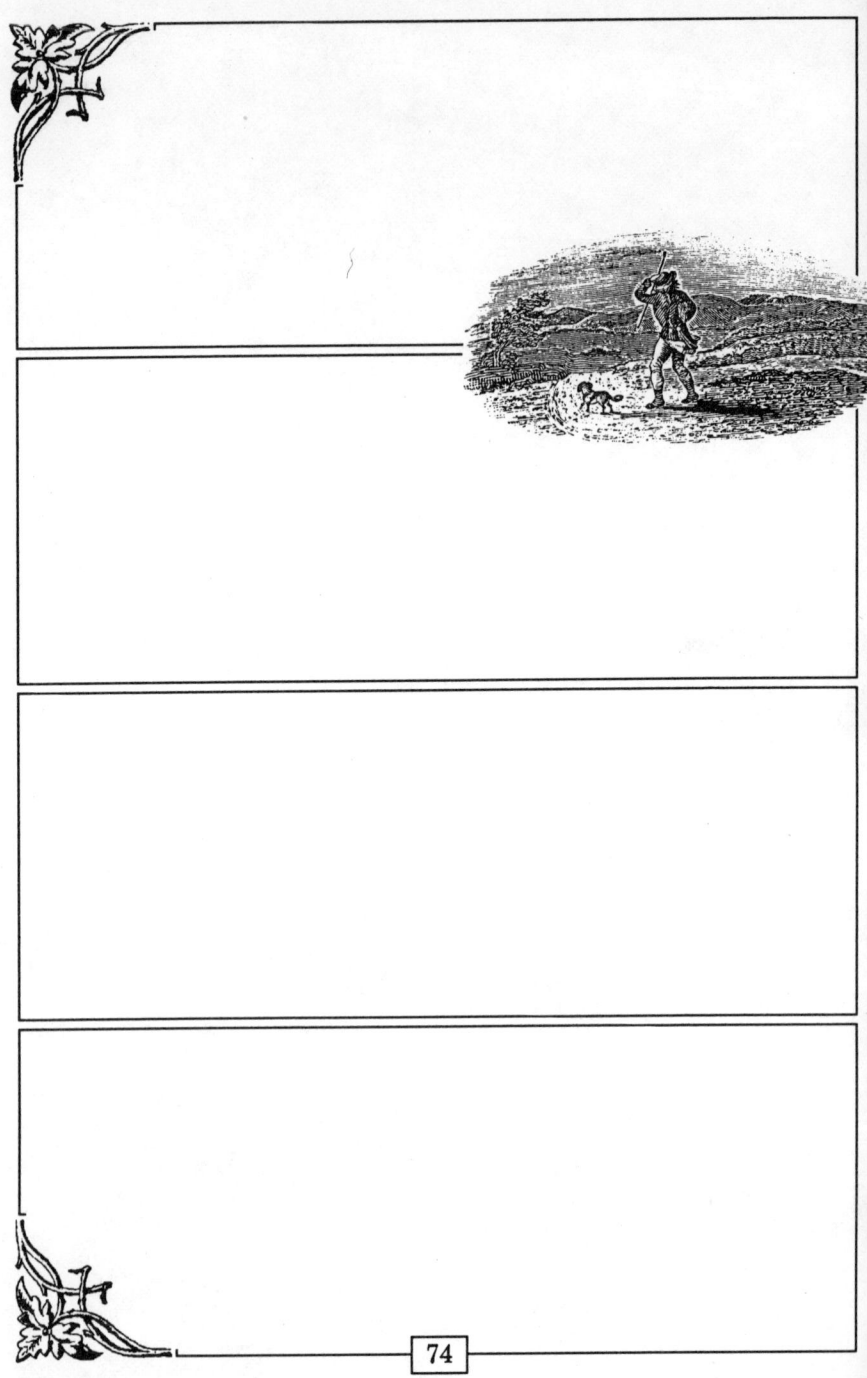

*A*utumn coloring is beginning to show. The elms grow rusty, and the nut trees, but the clematis blooms white by the wall, asters and goldenrod color the countryside, last fading proof of summer... The earliest autumn coloring along the country roads comes on woodbine and poison ivy... The cornflower is in bloom, the goldenrod is passing, the asters are at the height of their glory... Never, I think, have I seen the summer so deepen into maturity, such autumn days -- such serenity -- such placid beauty -- never as this year. **The Countryman's Year**

*A*utumn comes now, full of beauty, no killing frost at all, but warm, still, sunny days and cool nights full of peace. The apples are falling, the luscious plums, as large as peaches, hang yellow - ripe on the tree, the early pears are in and canned, the late [ones] I shall be gathering today. We have a world of grapes, and the melons are the best that ever I raised in my life.

The Countryman's Year

> *I was a long time learning how to take hold of nature... I cannot now remember the exact time of its beginning, a habit of repeating under my breath...fragmentary words and sentences describing what it was that I saw or felt at the moment... These words, afterward remembered, or even written down in the little book I sometimes carried in my pocket, seemed to awaken echoes, however faint, of the exaltation of that moment in the woods or fields, and enabled me to live twice where formerly I had been able to live but once.* **Great Possessions**

The best partners of solitude are books. I like to take a book in my pocket, although...often I never read a word in it. It is like having a valued friend with you, though you walk for miles without saying a word to him or he to you... subconsciously you are aware of what he is thinking and feeling about this hillside or that distant view... He never interrupts at inconvenient moments, nor intrudes his thoughts upon yours, unless you desire it... So it is with books. **Great Possessions**

One of the great rewards of living in the country is the opportunity as well as the privilege of getting thoroughly acquainted with one's neighbors. The richest rewards of life, after all, come of a man's intense awareness of his surroundings -- that is, the sense of beauty, if he enjoys the natural scene, and the delight in new and deeper understandings, if his chief interest is in his human associations... One may find adventure on any hillside, romance in any valley -- if he possess the eye to see it...
Under My Elm

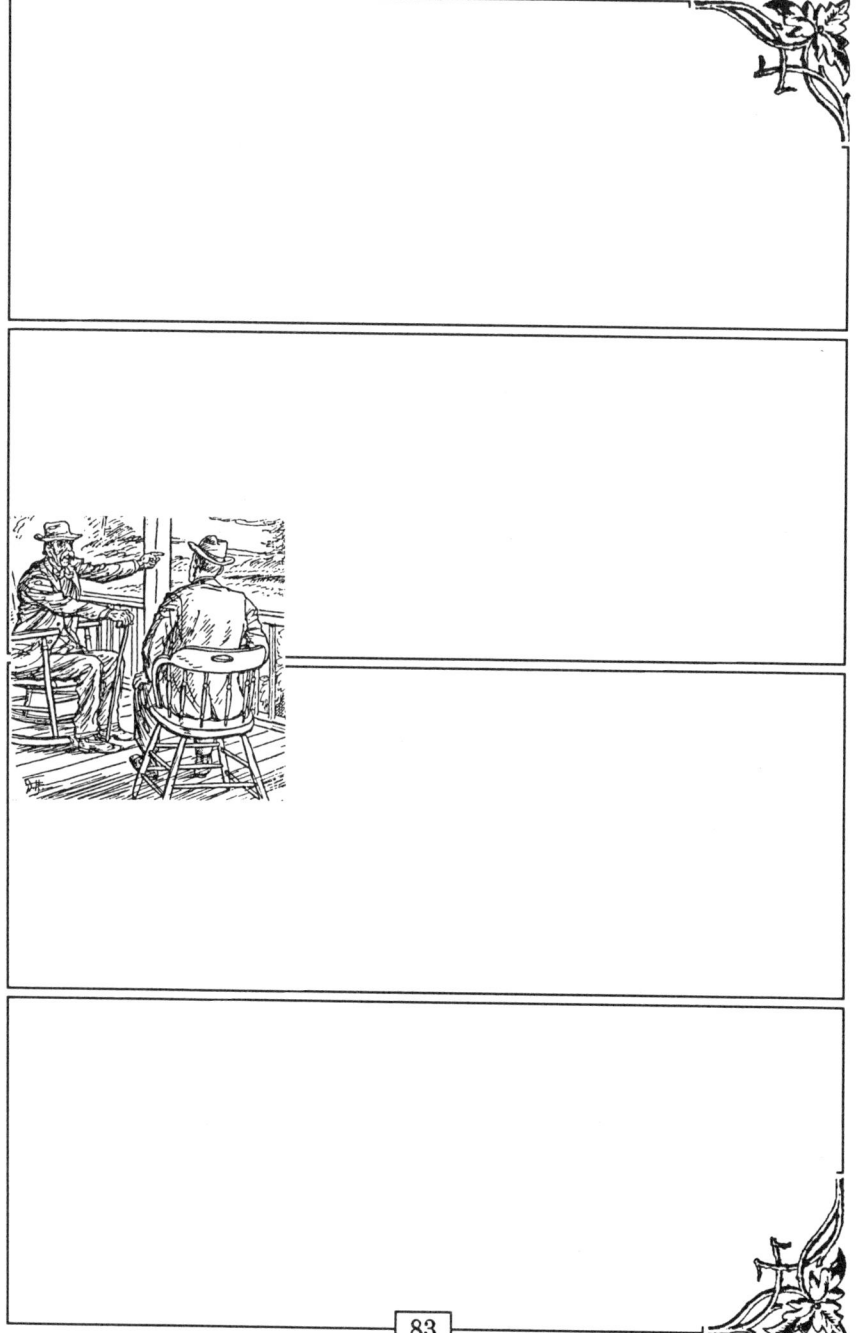

Autumn

I have been for a long tramp in country roads and with a kind of joy I cannot quite explain, since I heard nothing that could be sung on any stage, nor saw anything that could be published in any paper... A man currying a horse in a sunny barnyard and whistling as he worked... Fat bags of onions in long rows, tobacco hanging brown in open sheds, squashes and pumpkins piled high on sunny porches. Cows in the wide meadows. An enormous pig rooting in a potato field with unbounded unction, comfort, physical satisfaction in every grunt. I stopped there to laugh at him.

How easily accessible the really great rewards of life! One has only to step up and take them.

The Countryman's Year

...At a time like this when the whole world seems to be going mad -- when hatred and greed and fear and force are abroad in the world, and no end seems anywhere in sight... I keep thinking that the rejuvenation, when it comes, will come out of the land and the people who live freely, laboriously, productively, joyfully, upon it. What an anchor to windward in a storm like this now raging across the world! All stored property -- all stocks, bonds, all hived-up gold and silver, all paper wealth, may go off with the wind, but the land remains, and a man's faith in his own courage and strength.

Under My Elm

As I go out -- I hope not for long -- I wish you might follow me to the door, and then as we continue to talk quietly, I may beguile you, all unconsciously, to the top of the steps, or even find you at my side when we reach the gate at the end of the lane. I wish you might hate to let me go, as I myself hate to go! -- And when I reach the top of the hill (if you wait long enough) you will see me turn and wave my hand and you will know that I am still relishing the joy of our meeting, and that I part unwillingly.

Adventures in Friendship

*W*iney autumn mornings, clear and bright and still. I have just come in from a tramp in country roads to look at the new world... A perfect autumn morning, I delight in... the glory of the oaks not fully here. I found one of my apple trees full of starlings and stood watching them for a long time, listening to their delightful private conversation, interrupted from time to time by ironic whistling, no doubt at the enormity of the gossip that was going around.

The Countryman's Year

A perfect autumn day: New England at its best. I wish I could look long enough at the coloring on Mount Warner to keep it permanently in my inner eye. Such a tapestry of beauty: such sunlight: such crystal air! Was there ever anything finer? But if I really could retain it all, I might grow slothful with contentment, and another autumn, other golden and red tapestries, the wine of other Octobers, might fall upon a surfeited spirit.

The Countryman's Year

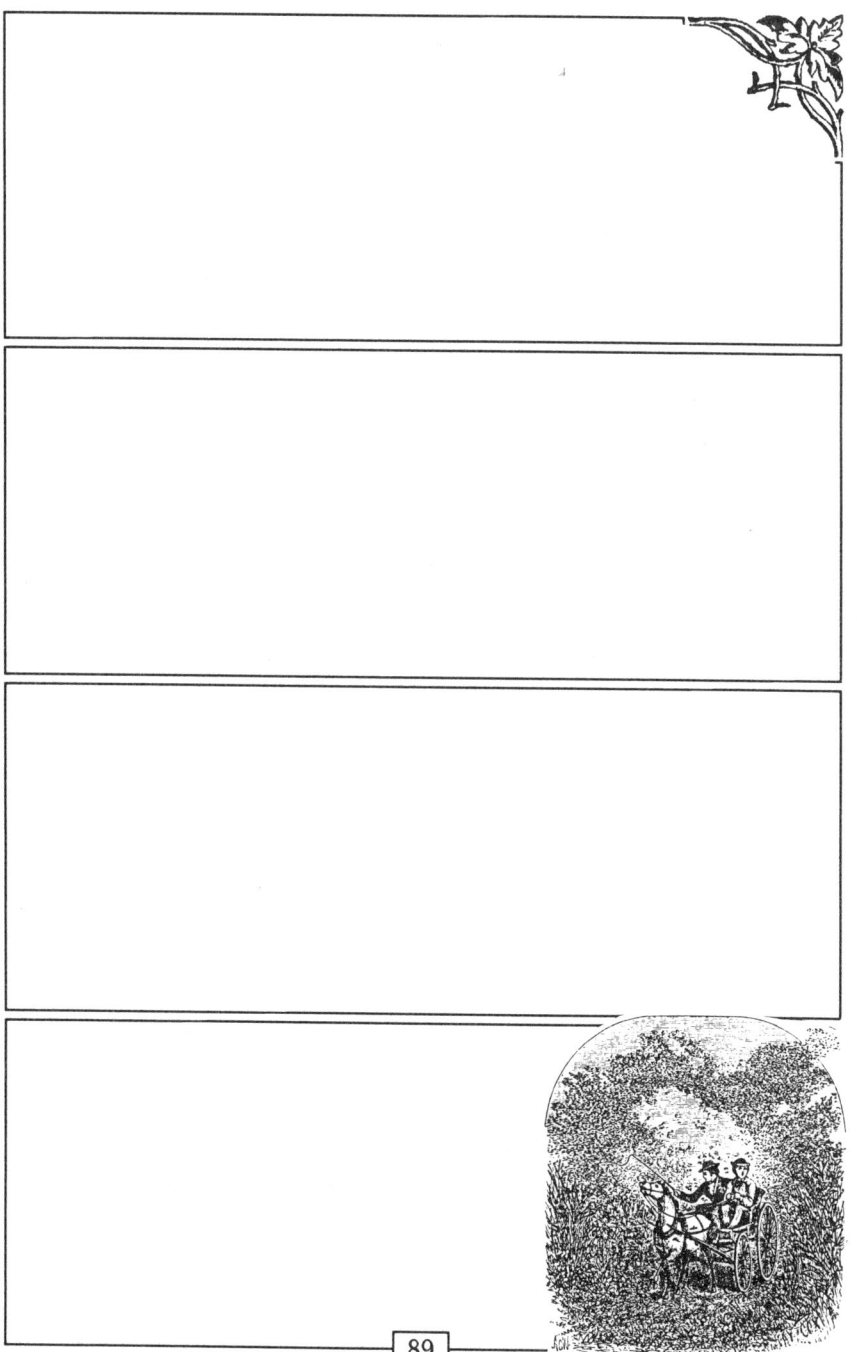

*N*ow come sunny mornings, cool and still, when the leaves drift downward through the sparkling air. No wind stirs them, no frost, no rain: it is the serene culmination of life. On such a day I can bear anything! ...These autumn days are beyond adjectives: every adjective I know seems leaden-footed when applied to mornings like these, or trusted to reveal the secret meaning of the hills, or interpret the message of the trees. I need verbs! Verbs to show what days like these <u>do</u> to a man's soul.

The Countryman's Year

> *O*ld Howieson...has posted all his fields with warnings against intrusion... I did not need to enter his fields, nor climb his hill, nor walk by his brook; but as the springs passed and the autumns whitened into winter, I came into more and more complete possession of all those fields he so jealously posted. ...I gathered rich crops -- and paid no taxes, worried over no mortgage, and often marvelled that he should be so poor within his posted domain and I so rich without.
>
> **Great Possessions**

> *The brilliant foliage of maples and ashes and most of the shrubs has disappeared, but the oaks are at their best... With the sun upon them...or shining through them, there are no more brilliant or thrilling reds and scarlets in all nature... On distant hills...the colors are subdued to deep rich bronzes shading down to brown, and where there is an intermingling of hemlocks or pines, the effect is a pageantry of color quite incomparable at any other time of year -- to me more satisfying in richness...than the gaudier coloring of early autumn.*
> **The Countryman's Year**

Working today with a quiet mind among my bees... The day has been fine and cool, all the world clad with sober gaiety in browns and tans and grays. All the leaves are down now, and the bareness is that of winter, yet the winter, upon a day like this of rich misty stillness, seems far off. I dismiss every consideration of my daily task -- all care banished -- and go about these simple affairs of my garden. Surely there are few things that better "still the beating mind."   **The Countryman's Year**

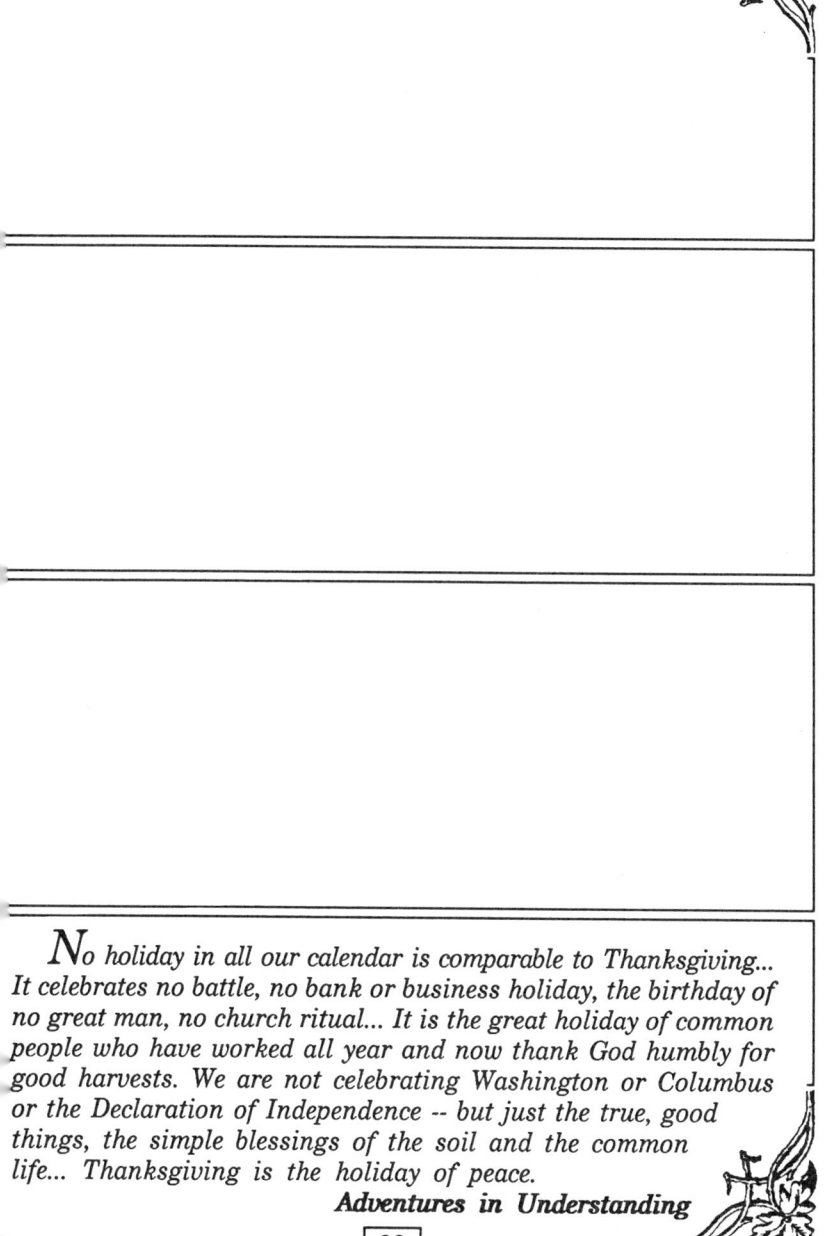

No *holiday in all our calendar is comparable to Thanksgiving... It celebrates no battle, no bank or business holiday, the birthday of no great man, no church ritual... It is the great holiday of common people who have worked all year and now thank God humbly for good harvests. We are not celebrating Washington or Columbus or the Declaration of Independence -- but just the true, good things, the simple blessings of the soil and the common life... Thanksgiving is the holiday of peace.*
Adventures in Understanding

I am impatient these days: there is not time enough in this one life. I need more lives; I have made plans already for three or four. I could easily expand to ten or twenty, all full-flavored, ardent, interesting. Full of curiosity! Looking into the sciences one after another, traveling to unexplored places, not only geographical, but psychological, social, economic; reading all the good books I do not yet know, and in all the languages; meeting every interesting human being then alive and with leisure -- with leisure! -- to know, to talk, to love. **Under My Elm**

All night the snow fell silently, without a breath of wind; the first real snow of the year. This morning a world clad in spotless white... What a time it is for turning inward: building a warm fire on the hearthstone of the spirit -- and sitting there on long still evenings to consider great things that have gone by, and greater things that are yet to come. A countryman's evening and the joys of it -- I could write an entire book to celebrate it!

The Countryman's Year

The best of these fine winter days, when the garden is full of snow, is my morning tramp in my old warm coat... The inner glow, the lift of the mind, as I tread the new snow with the sun coming up over the distant village! Life is good. I ask, indeed, why I am here, what it is all about, and have no answer, and yet how beautiful the wintry trees, how heady the morning air!

The Countryman's Year

I cannot tell how eagerly I tramped down the road that I might come quickly to the turning where I could catch the first glimpse of our own home... I made my way through a foot of unbroken snow to the doorway... I tramped it down and came thus into the dark, cold, strangely familiar house... I built up a little live blaze among the old ashes... and soon found myself presently singing, as I do when I am sure of my solitude. There is nothing like an open fire...to comfort the soul of man.
Adventures in Understanding

Christmas Day. Fierce cold, yet dry and clear, the snowy earth radiant with sunshine... We have skated on the pond, coasted on the hill, tramped the wintry roads -- and come in glowing, to shake ourselves out of coats and mufflers and seek the roaring open fires... The long table quite full, a tree that touched the ceiling, cries of astonishment and joy from all the little boys and girls, and many surprises and much laughter -- and music in the house -- and dancing. It has been a good Christmas Day.

The Countryman's Year

Somewhere on every farm, along with the other implements, there should be a row of good books, which should not be allowed to rust with disuse: a book, like a hoe, grows brighter with employment... What a convenient and delightful world is this world of books!... In this world every man is his own King...who has in his court the greatest men and women in the world... Invite any one of them to talk, and if your highness is not pleased with him you have only to put him back in his corner...

Adventures in Contentment

> *When I came to my farm from the city many years ago, it was as one...seeking to get hold again somewhere upon the realities of life... I that was worn out, bankrupt both physically and morally, learned to live again. I have achieved something of high happiness in these years, something I know of pure contentment... I have learned that happiness is not to be had for the seeking, but comes quietly to him who pauses at his difficult task and looks upward.*
>
> **The Friendly Road**

> *I do not know, truly, what we are here for upon this wonderful and beautiful earth, this incalculably interesting earth, unless it is to crowd into a few short years -- when all is said, terribly short years! -- every possible fine experience and adventure: unless it is to live our lives to the uttermost: unless it is to seize upon every fresh impression, develop every latent capacity: to grow as much as ever we have it in our power to grow.*
>
> **Great Possessions**

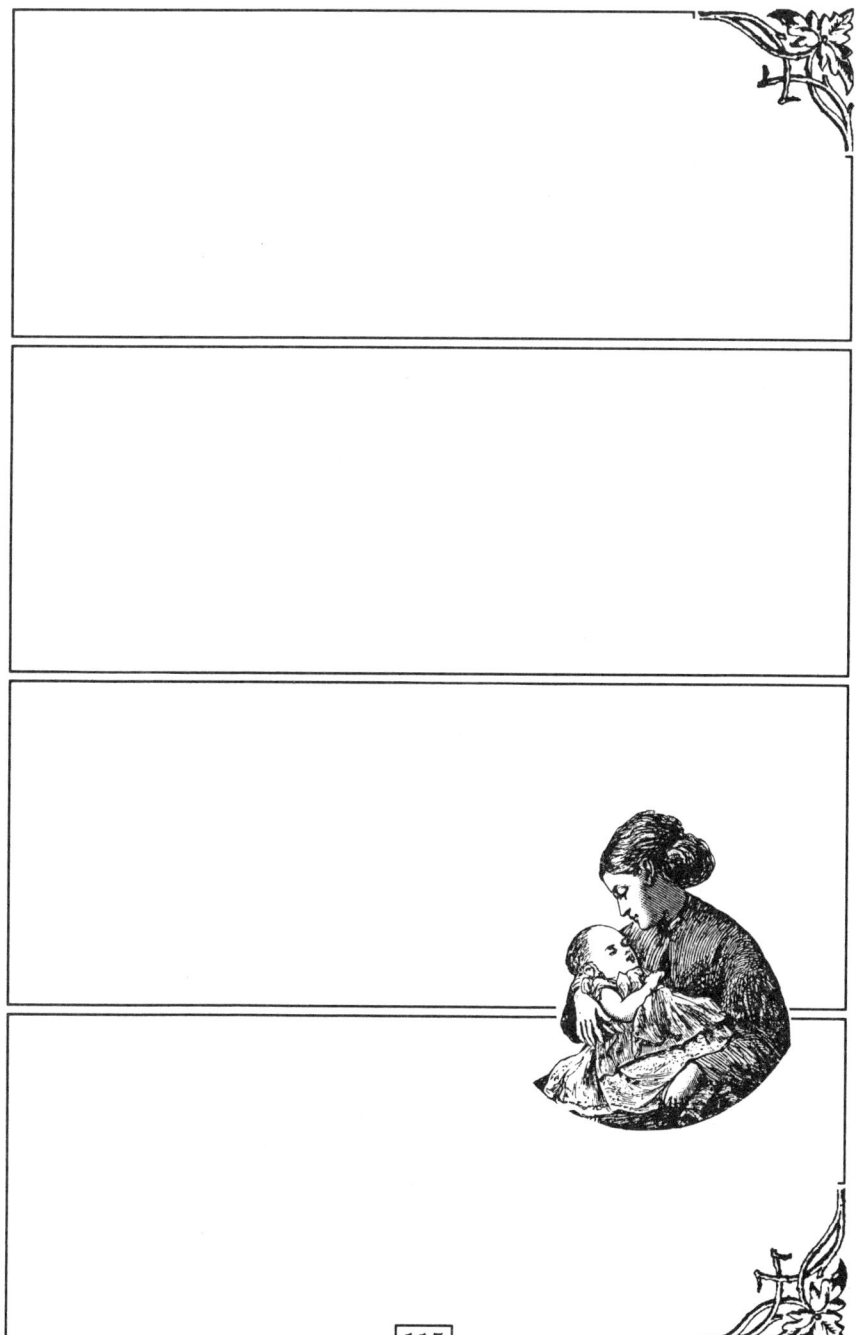

David Grayson was the pen name of accomplished turn-of-the-century journalist Ray Stannard Baker. Baker had a long, productive relationship with the prestigious *McClure's* magazine, bringing to its pages portraits of some of the day's geniuses: Theodore Roosevelt, Joel Chandler Harris, Stephen Crane, Admiral Dewey, Thomas A. Edison, Guglielmo Marconi. At a political gathering in January, 1910, he was enlightened by a speech from the president of Princeton University. Thus began the close friendship of Ray Stannard Baker and Woodrow Wilson, Baker following the future President throughout his administration and ultimately to Europe in 1918. He organized the press department at the Paris Peace Conference and reported the long, often bitter controversies over the League of Nations. Baker became Woodrow Wilson's official biographer and was awarded the Pulitzer Prize for his seven-volume *Woodrow Wilson: Life and Letters*.

David Grayson
(With his own *Country Journal?*)

But Ray Stannard Baker was a lover of quiet ways and simple pleasures: goals not easily attained in the hectic journalistic world. Thus emerged David Grayson, the writer in Baker who "wished most, if it can be expressed in a phrase, to be an introducer of human beings to one another, to be a maker of understandings." In pursuit of a more rational lifestyle, he moved his family to Amherst, Massachusetts, where they built their quiet, country dream home. From this refuge, Grayson recorded his daily thoughts and observations on the state of the farm, his neighbors, his bees, the nation and mankind.

David Grayson's Delightful ADVENTURES

ADVENTURES IN CONTENTMENT

Mentally and physically exhausted by his life as a city journalist, Grayson retreats to a small farm in Massachusetts.

"Through many feverish years I did not work: I merely produced... The only real thing I did was to hurry as though every moment were my last... Until I stopped I had not known the pace I ran."

ADVENTURES IN FRIENDSHIP

Grayson helps us re-discover, that plainest, commonest and rarest of things -- Friendship:

"A friend is one with whom we are fond of being when no business is afoot nor any entertainment contemplated. A man may well be silent with a friend."

ADVENTURES IN UNDERSTANDING

The Great War is on, and Grayson is called to serve, not with sword but with pen. The war effort means leaving his beloved Hempfield to return to The Wicked City. Yet as much as he disliked the move,

"In the City I came to understand many strange, new things about life and people, and the way to live."

ADVENTURES IN SOLITUDE

Through the pain and depression of a long hospitalization, Grayson discovers the inner strengths and resources that man possesses:

"(Though) everything that had constituted a pleasant and satisfying life for me...had been stripped away, I was still possessed of my own mind and my own thoughts. I had, after all, my own inner life. I had my life!"

Paperback w/jacket, $12.95 each   To Order call Toll Free 1-800-521-9221

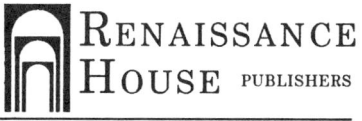

Renaissance House PUBLISHERS

541 Oak St. ~ P.O. Box 177
Frederick, CO 80530

Three More Classics by David Grayson

UNDER MY ELM

David Grayson looks back over 70 years at the things that have meant the most to him: his friends and family, his farm, his books, his trees and bees.

Paperback w/jacket, $12.95

THE COUNTRYMAN'S YEAR

A delightful day-by-day journey with Grayson through "the magic circle of the seasons." Grayson writes from his small New England farm where he says, "I have known the best that comes to any man..."

Paperback w/jacket, $12.95

A DAY OF PLEASANT BREAD

Here is Christmas the way you wish it were -- simple, plain, and heartful -- with just a pinch of New England humor. This delightful David Grayson tale takes us back to a time before glitz and glitter were the focal points of Christmas, when the fellowship of good people was the highlight of the day.

Paperback w/jacket & gift envelope, $5.95

To Order call Toll Free 1-800-521-9221

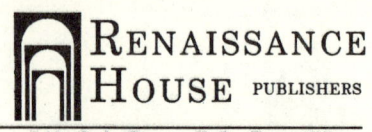
RENAISSANCE HOUSE PUBLISHERS

541 Oak St. ~ P.O. Box 177
Frederick, CO 80530